Wolfgang Amadeus
MOZART

TELL ME ABOUT

Wolfgang Amadeus
MOZART

by John Malam

❦ Carolrhoda Books, Inc. / Minneapolis

Carolrhoda Books, Inc., c/o The Lerner Publishing Group
241 First Avenue North, Minneapolis, Minnesota 55401 U.S.A.
Website address: www.lernerbooks.com

Library of Congress Cataloging-in-Publication Data

Malam, John.
    Wolfgang Amadeus Mozart / by John Malam.
        p.   cm. — (Tell me about)
    Includes index.
    Summary: A simple biography of the child prodigy who wrote more than
800 pieces of music before his untimely death at the age of thirty-five.
        ISBN 1-57505-247-4 (alk. paper)
    1. Mozart, Wolfgang Amadeus, 1756–1791—Juvenile literature.
2. Composers—Austria—Biography—Juvenile literature. [1. Mozart,
Wolfgang Amadeus, 1756–1791. 2. Composers.] 1. Series: Tell me about
(Minneapolis, Minn.)
ML3930.M9M27   1998
780'.92—dc21
    [B]   97-9246

Printed by Graficas Reunidas SA, Spain
Bound in the United States of America
1 2 3 4 5 6 – OS – 03 02 01 00 99 98

Wolfgang Amadeo Mozart   Wolfgang Amadeo Mozart

Wolfgang Amadeus Mozart was born in Salzburg about 250 years ago. Even as a child, he had a gift for writing music. He became a composer. Mozart became famous, but he never made very much money from his work. He died a young man. This is his story.

Wolfgang at fourteen. He is wearing a wig over his own hair, which was the fashion at the time.

Wolfgang was born in 1756. His parents were Leopold and Anna Maria Mozart. They had seven children, but five of them died. Only Wolfgang and his sister Maria Anna survived and grew up.

Maria Anna was four years older than Wolfgang. He called her by her nickname, Nannerl.

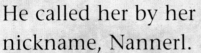

Wolfgang and his sister, Nannerl

The house in Salzburg, Austria, where Wolfgang was born was made into a museum.

6

Wolfgang was born into a world of music. His father wrote music and played the violin in the archbishop's orchestra. The archbishop was the ruler of Salzburg.

When Wolfgang was three, he would listen to Nannerl playing the clavichord. Soon he was playing it, too.

Wolfgang's father, Leopold

The house where young Wolfgang lived. He played on this clavichord, which is like a piano. He played the violin, too.

Leopold taught Wolfgang everything he could about music. Wolfgang could write music before he could write words. Leopold was proud of both his children, and he wanted people to know about them. This meant the family had to travel.

When Wolfgang was six, the Mozarts went to Vienna, the capital of Austria. There the children played for the royal family.

In Vienna, Wolfgang played for the emperor and empress.

8

The emperor called Wolfgang "a little wizard." The empress gave the Mozart children beautiful new clothes.

The Mozarts spent the next three years performing for royalty all over Europe. They returned home in 1766.

Wolfgang and Nannerl wearing the clothes the empress of Austria gave them

9

By the time Wolfgang was fourteen, he had written an opera and many other pieces of music. Some musicians were jealous. They said Wolfgang was too young to have written such wonderful music. They would not play it.

Wolfgang wrote this music in an exercise book when he was eight years old.

Sometimes people ate and talked while Wolfgang played. He didn't like playing for people who didn't pay attention.

10

As a teenager, Wolfgang composed music for the archbishop of Salzburg. When he was twenty-three, he took a job playing the organ in the archbishop's orchestra. The two men didn't get along, so Wolfgang left the orchestra.

Salzburg, where Wolfgang worked for the archbishop. Wolfgang played the organ in the cathedral.

Wolfgang went to Vienna, where he fell in love with Constanze Weber. She was a singer. They married when Wolfgang was twenty-six. The next year, they had a baby boy. Soon after the baby was born, the Mozarts went to Salzburg and left their son with a nanny. While they were away, the baby died.

Constanze, Wolfgang's wife

12

Wolfgang Amadeo Mozart Wolfgang Amadeo Mozart

Wolfgang and Constanze had five more children. Only two boys, Karl and Franz, survived. All their other children died.

The Mozarts bought fine clothes and held parties for their friends. They even had their own carriage, which was a great luxury in those days. They were always short of money.

Wolfgang's children Karl and Franz

Soon Wolfgang and Constanze could not afford to keep their apartment. They moved to a smaller place and then to another. Wolfgang wrote letters asking friends for money.

Wolfgang kept writing music. He wrote some of his best pieces at the hardest time of his life. One of Wolfgang's greatest operas was *The Marriage of Figaro,* finished in 1786. The opera was very popular, but Wolfgang earned only a small fee for the work.

A building in Vienna where Constanze and Wolfgang had an apartment

14

Wolfgango Amadeo Mozart

Between operas, he wrote other music, including symphonies and pieces for stringed instruments. He also taught music and performed. He worked hard but he did not earn much money.

The Marriage of Figaro is still a favorite opera.

People all over the world watch performances of Wolfgang's operas in opera houses like this one in Italy.

In 1791, Wolfgang wrote an opera called *The Magic Flute.* It is the story of a prince and princess who learn the difference between good and evil. It was a great success. Wolfgang also worked on a requiem, music played to honor a dead person. Later a count wanted to pretend he had written the *Requiem,* but Constanze made sure people knew it was Wolfgang's work.

A performance of Wolfgang's *Requiem* in a church in Austria

At the end of 1791, Wolfgang became very sick. He fainted a lot and had stomach pains. He thought his enemies had poisoned him, but many people think his kidneys failed. Doctors could do nothing to save him. Wolfgang died on December 5, 1791. He was thirty-five years old.

Wolfgang kept on writing music even when he was very sick.

Wolfgango Amadeo Mozart

The Mozarts were still poor when Wolfgang died, and Constanze could not afford much of a funeral. The great composer was buried in an unmarked grave, and no one knows where it is. It was a sad end for a man with so much talent. In Wolfgang's short life, he wrote more than six hundred pieces of music. It has been said that "the magic of his music lights the darkness of people's lives."

This memorial to Mozart is in Vienna. The broken column shows that Mozart's life was cut short.

W A MOZART

1756 1791

In 1996, a great discovery was made in the United States. Part of a song written by Mozart was found in an attic. No one knows how it got there. People were very excited to hear the song. It was the first time it had been heard in more than two hundred years.

The music that was found in an attic

The part of the song that was found takes only one minute to sing. The rest is still missing.

19

Important Dates

1756 Wolfgang Amadeus Mozart born in Salzburg

1759 Began to play the clavichord

1761 Wrote his first piece of music

1762 Left on first music tour

1764 Wrote his first symphony

1766 Returned home from tour of Europe

1769 Traveled to Italy with father

1770 His first opera performed

1777 Left for Paris with mother

1778 Mother died

1779 Joined archbishop of Salzburg's orchestra

1781 Left orchestra

1782 Married Constanze Weber

1784 Son Karl born

1786 Wrote *The Marriage of Figaro*

1787 Father died

1791 Wrote *The Magic Flute*

Son Franz born

Wolfgang Amadeus Mozart died

Key Words

clavichord
a keyboard instrument that is an ancestor of the piano

composer
a person who writes music

opera
a play in which most of the lines are sung rather than spoken

orchestra
a group of musicians who play together on many different instruments

requiem
a piece of music written to honor someone who has died

symphony
a piece of music written for an entire orchestra to play

A statue of Mozart in Salzburg

Index

Archbishop of Salzburg, 7, 11

Birth 5, 6

Children, 12, 13

Death, 5, 17, 18

Early talent, 5, 7, 8, 10

Francis I (Holy Roman
  Emperor), 8, 9

Magic Flute, The, 16
Maria Theresa (empress of
  Austria), 8, 9
Marriage, 12
Marriage of Figaro, The, 14, 15
Memorial, 18
Money, 5, 13, 14, 15, 18
Mozart, Anna Maria
  (mother), 6
Mozart, Constanze Weber
  (wife), 12, 13, 14, 16, 18
Mozart, Franz (son), 13
Mozart, Karl (son), 13
Mozart, Leopold (father), 6,
  7, 8

Mozart, Maria Anna
  (Nannerl) (sister), 6, 7, 8, 9
Operas, 10, 14, 15, 16

Performing, 9, 11, 15
Popularity, 5, 14, 16, 18, 19

Requiem, 16

Salzburg, 5, 6, 7, 9, 11, 12

Traveling, 8, 9

Vienna, 8, 12, 14, 18

Acknowledgments

The author and publisher gratefully acknowledge the following for permission to reproduce copyrighted material:

Cover AKG

page 5 AKG **page 6** (left) Robert Harding Picture Library (right) Mozart Museum, Salzburg/Bridgeman Art Library **page 7** AKG **page 8** AKG **page 9** AKG **page 10** (top) Image Select (bottom) Chateau de Versailles/Giraudon/Bridgeman Art Library **page 11** (top) Rolf Richardson/Robert Harding Picture Library **page 12** AKG **page 13** Mozart Museum, Salzburg/Bridgeman Art Library **page 14** Historisches Museum der Stadt, Vienna **page 15** Robert Harding Picture Library **page 16** Image Select/Ann Ronan **page 17** AKG **page 18** AKG **page 19** (top) Christie's Images (bottom) Des Jenson/Times Newspapers Limited **page 21** AKG

About the Author

John Malam has a degree in ancient history and archeology from the University of Birmingham in England. He is the author of many children's books on topics that include history, natural history, natural science, and biography. Before becoming a writer and editor, he directed archeological excavations. Malam lives in Manchester, England, with his wife, Hilary, and their children, Joseph and Eve.